CLOSE TO HOME
REVISITED

Other Close to Home books by John McPherson

Close to Home
One Step Closer to Home
Dangerously Close to Home

Close to Home: A Book of Postcards

Also by John McPherson

High School Isn't Pretty

Close to Home
Revisited

By John McPherson

ANDREWS AND McMEEL
A UNIVERSAL PRESS SYNDICATE COMPANY
KANSAS CITY

For Scott

Many thanks to Peggy McKeehan for her superb watercoloring of cartoons throughout this book.

John McPherson

"Apparently I have done something to upset you."

"Tell us about the time you blocked the field goal and saved the big game against Penn State, Grandpa."

"The dog ate my headphones."

Going to the same school as your younger brother can be an agonizing experience.

"I hate it when it's Ohler's turn to drive."

"Dan backed over the stroller in the driveway."

WHIRR!

"I'll be there in a second, dear. I'm tucking the kids in."

"Sorry about the mix-up, Mr. Bixford. We'll be moving you to a semi-private room shortly."

"Lucy, I think we need to have a talk about
this little stenciling project of yours."

"Uhh ... Excuse me, ma'am, but you've ...
uh ... taken my cart by mistake.
I believe that's yours there."

"Yeah, I know she shouldn't play with her food.
But that's pretty good!"

"You wouldn't believe the money we save by buying remnants."

"Whatever happened to the days when you could just tie an old tire to a tree branch?"

Working for the No. 1 manufacturer of bean-bag chairs does have its downside.

"Bill! We've got a problem in here with the spin cycle!!"

15

"That settles it! No catnip for *that* cat!"

"Oh, isn't that *darling*! She's telling you how old she is!"

WELL, I THINK LOIS RAISES A GOOD POINT.

Budget conference call

"Stick the other end of this in your mouth and say 'Ahh.'"

"So, is this your first baby?"

"And then the mean mommy took the kind daddy's golf clubs and broke them all in half. "Clean the garage!" she roared, as smoke poured from her nostrils."

FRANK!

"I don't know how we got by before we had the automatic teller machine installed."

"He's got such interesting markings!"

"Ryan's walking two months earlier than most other kids, thanks to these training shoes that Gary made in the basement."

Purchasing a new phone these days can
spark some heated negotiations.

How to toddler-proof your home.

"Roger, we've been over this before. I need my closet space.
Besides, there's more room for your clothes down here."

"I'll give you five bucks if you'll put eight miles on this thing before your father gets home."

"Sorry, Mom. I thought I had enough momentum to clear the house."

"OK! Who's the wise guy who put the Mr. Yuk sticker on my turnip casserole?!"

"We're having a little trouble with our scanners. Just divide our total by 37.21."

"I've been bugging Roger forever to have central air conditioning installed, but he insists that we don't need it."

"Ready to *work* at 8 o'clock, Velez! Not just *here* at 8 o'clock! Ready to work!"

"According to this scale, I've lost seven pounds just from walking around the carnival!"

"Do me a favor and act like there's nothing wrong with it. My dad's pretty proud of the fact that he put it together all by himself."

"Here's part of an old cheeseburger, and I think I can feel a couple more french fries."

23

"Wonderful news, George! Your cousin Freddie got a job selling vinyl siding!"

"I don't like the looks of this storm."

"I can't believe you spent 150 bucks for those rollerblades when I was able to make these for less than 30 bucks!"

Unfortunately, Bernice didn't read the washing instructions on her new blouse until she got it home.

As the band continued to play, an angry mob searched for members of the prom committee.

"We wanted to get him one of those marble-tower kits, but we were worried that he might swallow a marble."

"This is my new recycling system."

"How ironic! You walk 9 miles in 90 degree heat to borrow some coat hangers, struggle for 2 1/2 hours to open the door, and here I've had a spare set of keys in my purse the whole time."

A lot of people feel that the personalized-check rage is getting out of hand.

Walt Nordman was not a morning person.

"How many times do I have to tell you kids to stop giving each other shocks? You're scuffing up my rug!"

28

"For cryin' out loud, just pick one!
He's never going to recognize it!"

The agony of living with a cold-footed spouse.

"We get 984 channels now, thanks to this new cable."

"Can't you do something for this static cling?"

How to make your wife hysterical

"I want to apologize to all of you for the side effects caused by last week's lab."

NUTS!

PLINK!

THUNK!

"Let's see now ... driver's license, driver's license ... could you hold this, too? Driver's license, driver's license ... describe it to me again. ..."

Just a typical morning for a one-bathroom couple.

"You got any bright ideas how to get a peanut butter and jelly sandwich out of the VCR?"

"And this little piggy faked left and ran up the middle for a 28-yard gain."

"The best part of it is I made this quilt entirely out of materials I found around the house."

Peggy's chances of getting a second date with Jack Mangiante took a turn for the worse when her dad started playing the theme to "Gilligan's Island" on his teeth.

The growing interest in health and fitness has had an effect on even the longest-standing traditions.

33

"Down boy!"

"I haven't gotten to that part yet!"

"I'll take six hamburgers, four small fries, four Cokes, and a hundred napkins."

"Unbelievable! I pump 14 tubes of caulk into a 3-inch gap in the siding and it's still not filled up!"

Research has shown that wearing a
baseball cap backwards lowers one's
IQ by as much as 50 points.

"For Pete's sake, will you take that ridiculous
wig off her?! It is perfectly normal for a
6-month-old to have no hair!"

Friends of the Norblocks were beginning to
sense some tension between Ed and Helen.

"What am I doing? I'm making this
two-pronged outlet into a
three-pronged outlet."

"I was just standing there in the yard when Art Nabro threw a snowball at me. So I threw one back. Then he threw a bigger one back at me. I threw an even *bigger* one back at him ... "

"Oh, nothing. I just finished resealing the driveway and Ann is out getting some groceries. What's up with you?"

"And here's a little piece of equipment you're going to get to know *real* well, Danny. That's it, get used to the feel of the handle. Good!"

"Hey, you want her to sleep through
the night, don't you?"

"Mom, he is *not* a date! Danny and I are just friends."

"Leave the kitty alone, dear."

"Check it out. I've been cutting a half-inch off Dad's chair legs every day for the last two weeks."

"Freshwater pearls? No! These are the kids' baby teeth!"

"Most people find this hole particularly challenging."

"The toy manufacturers finally got smart and came up with a puzzle that kids can't lose the pieces to."

"This is *not* what I had in mind when I said I wanted us to add a master bathroom!"

"Once again, I want to stress that the story I just related during my sermon is *purely* fictional and is no way based upon anyone here in the congregation."

"I admit, I was apprehensive when Alan first talked about getting an industrial-strength garbage disposal, but now I don't know how we got by without it."

Algebra teacher Bert Fegman was a master of reverse psychology.

Mike would know better than to raise his hand
the next time Mr. Ferncod asked for a
volunteer to erase the blackboard.

"Here you go, right on page 13 of the
manual: 'Never stop walking while
the treadmill is on.'"

"Hey, Dad. I heard an interesting story. Did you know that Einstein failed math?! Really, it's true! Pretty amazing, huh, Dad?! Smart guy like Einstein doing crummy at math."

"How much longer are you going to be on this diet?"

"There! You felt it kick *that* time, didn't you?"

"You kids drive me nuts! All day long you pester me about ice cream and now you aren't hungry!"

"Sorry, Steve. It looks like you're closest to the garter."

"I do *not* want you feeding the dog scraps
at the dinner table!"

"That's exactly what he wants you to do, Al.
Can't you see this is just a ploy to get attention?
Don't give him the satisfaction of knowing
that his behavior upsets you."

Every high school student's worst enemy:
the essay question.

"I fell asleep in the tub."

"How 'bout those crazy jet streams?!"

A hot new fad: the party skateboard

"Oh, nonsense! It doesn't look silly at all!
When you've got a head cold as bad as
yours, it's important to be prepared!"

One of the 10 warning signs that the
honeymoon is over.

The Menlop brothers drop their dad some
subtle hints that they want a bigger TV.

"Stan, will you knock it off!
He will walk when he's ready to walk!"

"Wow! First a drum and now cymbals!
Thanks, Grandma and Grandpa!"

"You'll get your $50 deposit back as long as
you bring Darlene home by midnight."

"What are the chances I could get a $7,000 advance on my allowance?"

"All right now, give Mommy the super-glue."

BLAT!

"We couldn't find any rice, so we're using mashed potatoes instead."

"I think we'll all be relieved when this rain lets up."

"That's a false eyelash."

The '90s dad: able to spend time with his kids
while still indulging in his favorite sport.

"I got some of that hair that comes in a spray can, but I wanted to test it on the dog first."

It's never hard to spot the spouses at the annual office Christmas party.

"I told my parents I had to have a phone in my room, so they moved all my stuff into the living room."

The Older Generation fights back.

"Now what have I told you? *Never* bother Mommy
when she's in the bathroom!"

"We were running out of room for the kids' drawings
so we had to get another refrigerator."

Never let your parents chaperone
a school dance.

"See you had a little problem with the weed eater."

Though he was a star on the school's soccer team, Les Babko was having a tough time with baseball.

"In the last couple of months, we've noticed a big improvement in her motor skills."

"Darlene, what a clever gift idea! A dress shirt made entirely out of bread wrapper twist ties! You can wear it to your big meeting on Friday, Wayne!"

"It helps me to unwind."

"The funny thing is, Dad, I was only going 10 miles an hour when it happened."

"Are you sure you checked out this place's references?"

"Vern considers it a sign of weakness if he empties
the grass bag before he's finished the lawn."

"Sometimes I worry that your mom doesn't get enough exercise."

Bud saved a bundle by making Christmas gifts for his family in metal shop.

"We kept losing the other remote."

"Yes, it is kind of like having a giant puppet. Now let Daddy get some sleep. You can play with him again after lunch."

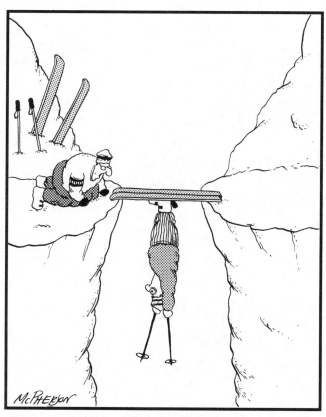

"You better get those bindings checked out when you get back to the lodge. Those things should have released after a wipeout like this."

In a matter of seconds, Steve's social life was reduced to that of pond scum.

"And over here's our family snow shovel. This baby can clear a driveway in no time."

"The kid in 4C got a BB gun for Christmas."

Mrs. Mortleman made sure that everyone participated in class.

Suddenly, Diane realized the incredible power
that she had.

"It's recycled aluminum siding."

"Here it is! Glerf! It means 'Oprah's on'!"

"I forgot to bring my notebook to algebra today."

Wayne Pelnard was obsessed with winning the $10,000 prize on
"America's Funniest Home Videos."

"For cryin' out loud! Would you just take a
sick day for once in your life!"

Ranch houses have taken some of the thrill
out of eloping.

"No, that's not what I said. I said I made a New Year's resolution not to eat dinner in my underwear *when your mother is here.*"

"OK, let's have one more shot. This time, try not to look directly at the flash."

"It just got to the point where it was impossible to keep track of all the kids, so Dan had the control center installed."

How to stop a blanket hog.

"Hey, Mike, I think you forgot your lunch again."

"Yeah, I know your contractions are only two minutes apart. But if you can just hang in there until tomorrow, I'll win the baby pool at work."

"I am *not* doting on you! I just want you to look good for your big meeting, hon. Now let me fix this collar."

"You must have dozed off for quite a while."

"I've told you a hundred times! Always check the lawn for foreign objects before you mow!"

Budget wedding photos

How to embarrass your spouse.

Students weren't too fond of the
new enlarged report cards.

"Oh, Delores, you lucky girl!
You caught the bouquet!"

Unable to find a Hi-Liter, Wayne Merlman
used a black Magic Marker to cross out all
the stuff he didn't want to read again.

"My burger's still a little pink on the inside.
Hold the cigarette lighter up to it for a
couple of minutes, would ya?"

At the Minivan Owners Support Group

"Dee Dee Vershay's dog is having a hernia operation. Everybody's signing this get-well card and kicking in $10."

How to get a teen-ager to mow the lawn.

"Well, thank you, Wayne and Elwin. An Assault of the Psycho Slime Monsters Nintendo cartridge. How thoughtful of you."

"According to our data, a small hole in the ozone layer has opened up directly above your house."

"The dog ate the remote again."

"All I can say is, next time I'll know better when somebody offers me a free car phone for just opening a new checking account."

"There's no such thing as the Toenail Fairy, bonehead!"

Vern messes up his right-turn signal again.

Despite an 0-and-14 season and slumping attendance, loyal Pigeons fans still showed their support by doing the Wave.

"I'm concerned about his thumbsucking."

Louis Wrzynski's lifelong fascination with dominoes culminated in this one fateful moment.

"You want your dessert now or later?"

"Wow! That was neat, Dad! OK, teach me how to throw it! Dad?!"

"His high school reunion is tomorrow."

"Watch your step going through the living room.
Lloyd got a little confused when it came to
installing the new ceiling fan."

Ted felt it was important to have a resume that
would catch the personnel manager's eye.

"My typewriter broke, so I had to do my term
paper on the Etch A Sketch."

"And so, in appreciation of his suggestion, which will save the company more than $350,000 annually, I am honored to present Al Wimbot with this exquisite stainless-steel tire gauge, engraved with the company's logo!"

"With five kids in the house, this was the only way we could think of to give everybody a fair shot at the bathroom."

"All right! Who's the dingbat who used the phone last?!"

Vern had yet to master the art of first-date conversation.

"Psst! Make sure you get her home by midnight!"

Norm Pitloff would go to any length to use the car pooling lane.

"I don't think you need to push quite so hard, Dad."

"I couldn't find a ladder."

"The rest of the bell choir is out with the flu."

"Wonderful. We spend $200 on toys and she plays with a shoe box for three days non-stop."

"This darned icemaker is on the fritz."

"Thank heavens this vacuum has a reverse button!"

"Talk about perfect timing! I just happened to walk out here with the camcorder just as that rung broke!"

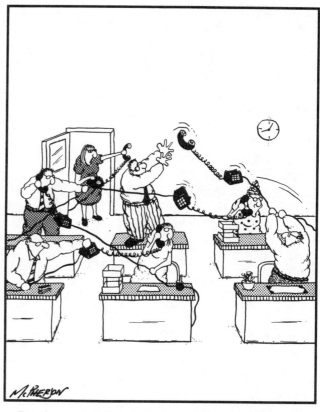

Employees at Bumfarb Associates hadn't quite mastered the fine art of transferring phone calls.

Friends had warned Bert not to join a CD club.

"There! Now you've got no reason to wake us up
at 3 a.m. asking for a glass of water."

"Hey, what do you care?
They give you free refills."

"Some guy from the Department of Public Works
came over and installed it this morning.
The city's trying to raise enough money
for a new skating rink."

"Whoops! Sorry I missed that rest area. Oh, well.
The sign says there's another one in 76 miles."

Many first-time fathers take the job of videotaping the birth far too seriously.

"I thought you said you fixed the problem with the blow dryer."

Get even with guests who snoop in your medicine cabinet. Fill it with marbles before your next party.

"I want to start getting used to this backpack before the baby comes along."

"I hope this is just some kind of cruel joke, Dad!"

As a courtesy to their fellow joggers, more and more people are starting to wear mudflaps.

New employees were quick to notice the little cliques that existed at the P. L. Fernley Co.

"Yep, I got this beauty used from that amusement park over in Elmira. Made out like a bandit!"

"Their 4-year-old just got potty-trained."

"Howard, I'm cold. Put on two more cats."

"Oh, look at this! Our little girl coming home from her first date! You kids just go ahead and say good night as though we're not even here!"

"Did somebody here call about too much air conditioning blowin' on their head?"

How to humiliate your husband

Unable to decide on a name for their baby,
Steve and Kim Robb leave it to fate.

"Hey! I'm picking up another real strong signal
here! Gotta be at least a half-dollar! Heh heh!
We need to have the Schmitts over more often!"

"Can you feel the Novocain yet?"

"Elaine's been bugging me for years to give
her more closet space."

"Here's another one of Rowena waving! That's the World Trade Center in the background, and if you look closely ..."

NUMBER FOUR, CAN YOU ANSWER THAT QUESTION FOR US?

Mr. Gickman wasn't too good with names.

"Here's something that should knock out that head cold. I got you some of that new deep sinus decongestant."

"For total biking realism, here's our finest exercise bike, complete with a growling dog, a tape deck that plays rude comments from motorists, and this nozzle which emits a fine mist of bugs."

Lisa's dad had a surefire method for getting her downstairs in time for dates.

"What are you mad at me for? He loves this! Plus this terrycloth outfit he's wearing is perfect for waxing the car."

"Sorry about this. My mom's a little bit paranoid when it comes to stuff like sparklers."

"You can come out now, Mrs. Ziffler. Ron caught
Howie and locked him in his room. Say,
if you're free Friday night, we'd love
to have you baby-sit again."

Chuck and Pete don't let the fact that they
live in Kansas stop them from experiencing
the thrills of surfing.

94

"OK! Put the dead spider in that cube, the centipede there, and the chipmunk foot in that one. Then we stick the tray in the freezer and watch the expressions on everybody's faces at Mom and Dad's big party Saturday night!"

"Must be the pizza delivery kid that we forgot to tip last week."

"I can never remember to water those darned plants."

"Well, we hope you slept good. Believe it or not, we picked that
sofa bed up at a garage sale for only $50!"

"Are you trying to destroy my social life?
I know people around here, Dad!
Please take off that stupid hat!"

"How's the wild rice?"

"Get the red Buick in the third row."

"This stupid thing is clumping up again."

"Phil did all of the plumbing in the house entirely by himself."

"This isn't what I had in mind when I requested a semi-private room."

"I guess maybe now my canine ankle fences
don't look so stupid, huh, wise guy?!"

"Yep, here it is right in the lease:
'Refrigerator shall be shared equally between
tenants in apartments 4A and 4B.'"

The S.A.T.: the ultimate test of a
student's intelligence.

"OK! Cover me!"

"Why on earth can't you learn to pull up closer?!"

Fortunately, Eleanor was able to get a full refund from the computer dating service.

"Jerry, the Morrison kid is here. He wants to know if we offer a health plan in addition to the five bucks we're paying him to mow the lawn."

Where doctors keep their stethoscopes.

"Sorry about that little power outage there. We were installing an electric air freshener in the men's room. Hope we didn't mess up yer data or whatever yer doin' there."

"This isn't what I was expecting when they asked us over to see their slides."

"I tell you! These hide-a-key rocks are just the cleverest things!"

"Look, I know you hate it, but until I get a chance to put some non-slip decals in the tub, I'd feel a lot better if you'd just wear the helmet."

"My 17-year-old drove the car into the garage door three times, so I finally just said the heck with it and installed the beads."

Marge had worked out a little signal to let her husband know when he was spending too much time in the shower.

"Are you serious? Your dad actually put a meter on the TV and if we want to watch the rest of 'Beverly Hills 90210' we need to put in $1.75?"

Thus far, Frank wasn't too impressed with the company's dental plan.

"We know this is a bit unusual, Mrs. Glenmont. But since we've never hired a baby sitter before, I'm sure you can understand that we're just taking some precautions."

104

Birthday-phobia, Stage One: Denial

"Go!"

"It only takes me about four minutes to paint the entire house, but it's a pain in the neck cleaning this thing when I'm done."

The ever-annoying Naugahyde-in-summer syndrome.

"Oh, for heaven's sake! It's Stan and Lois Murdock from New Year's weekend!"

Charlene soon began to realize that being the teacher's pet wasn't all it was cracked up to be.

"Oh, Wait! Here's the problem! The hose was kinked!"

"You know, they always say that 80 percent of all accidents happen at home."

"I am waxing the car! What does it *look* like I'm doing?"

Despite their popularity, many of the fancy new mall hair salons just don't have the
personal touch of the old neighborhood barber shops.

"Man! That was one *mean* pothole!"

"For cryin' out loud, if you like the smell of the
cologne in the ad, go out and buy some of it!"

"Leaving handprints is for wimps!"

"I made these out of leftovers from Thanksgiving dinner. They're gravy Popsicles."

Despite the popularity of biking shorts,
only about three percent of the population
actually looks good wearing them.

Chuck wasn't about to let another ground
ball roll through his legs.

"That settles it! Next car we buy has to
have cloth seats!"

"Maybe our price is too high."

"Not only is it good exercise for Bob, it's also great entertainment for the kids."

"Try jiggling the handle."

"Nah, it's still not quite right. Put in more worms."

"We're trying to streamline things around here."

"I figured out that 478 times around the table is a mile."

"We need to do something about this wax build-up."

"I don't care if the camp got an incredible deal on this thing by buying it secondhand from Wacky World. It still gives me the creeps."

Although the new office cubicles were a refreshing change, they did make it difficult to have a private conversation.

"I've been after Bob for years to have a screened porch installed. But when he showed me a cost comparison between a porch and mosquito netting, I had to agree that the netting made a lot more sense."

"It gets 169 miles per gallon, but it's sort of a pain when it comes to dating and getting groceries."

At a track meet in New Jersey.

Most newlyweds have a tendency to try to avoid any conflicts.

"Wow! I haven't heard Dad scream that loud
since we carved our names into the
hood of his Corvette!"

A behind-the-scenes look at people who
pair up college roommates.

"This one is the basic cable box, this one is for
upgraded service, then we've got HBO with this box,
this one is for the 24-hour fly-fishing channel, and
then of course the Vegetarian Channel,
the Monster Truck channel ..."

"Vern and I have very different tastes when it comes to decorating, but we've been able to compromise pretty well."

"That's what we get for buying the cheapest brand of fabric softener."

"Are you sure this is the honeymoon suite?"

"Sorry about the mix-up with the keyboards. We hope this won't affect your programming abilities."

"He does not have a discipline problem! He's just had a little too much sugar, that's all."

"Somebody finally got smart and came up with an above-ground pool that's got a deep end and a shallow end."

"The batteries to the remote are getting weak."

"How's Drew doing? Is he still up?"

"I have to give myself a lot of the blame.
I gave Dave a book called *How to Build
Your Own Deck* for Father's Day."

"Watch your step. There's quite a
drop-off over here."

"I had to do 95 the whole way back on the interstate, but I got Darla home by midnight like you wanted, Mr. Lampley."

The downside of going on a two-week vacation.

"All right, Dad! Now try *four* meatballs!"

"I want an action-adventure film, she wants a romantic comedy.
I just don't see how we can resolve this!"

"For the last time, no, you may not have your
own phone for the backseat!"

Frank and Vern would go to any length
to get the free lunch deal.

"Operator, get me the chocolate abuse hotline!"

"Sorry, sir. We've still got a few bugs to work out."

"Now, here's the funny part, Dad."

"This is *not* what I had in mind when I asked
you to take the baby for a stroll."

"So, tonight's the night you meet your future
in-laws, eh? Whoops! Sorry about that."

"That's another great thing about having a sunroof! It gives us the ability to fit into much tighter parking spots!"

How to tell when it's time to wash your gym socks.

Obviously, Carol needed more than simply dinner out to give her a break from taking care of her four kids.

"Well, my husband and I talked it over and agreed that it just isn't practical for us to own a sports car, so we decided it was best to sell it."

"Are you gonna make me return the chemistry set?"

"You must have punched in the wrong four-digit number."

"You'll probably find this considerably more strenuous
than other treadmill tests you've taken."

"Psycho? He's a Pekingese. This is all just for effect to ward off burglars!"

"Hey! Can they do that?!"

"For the last time, we are *not* buying an exercise bike!"

A cure for snoring

"Two or three months ago I was always exhausted
because he needed constant attention.
Now that he's able to entertain himself,
life is *so* much easier."

"If there's anything Ray can't stand,
it's raking leaves."

"I think I found the problem.
We left out a period."

"He cost a thousand bucks,
but he's one of a rare breed that knows
how to empty its own litter box."

"My Uncle Leon left us his Elvis chair
and matching lamp."

"When I got done, I discovered there had been a cockroach on the sunlamp the whole time."

"This just seemed to make a lot more sense. Now we just take out the mail we want and leave the rest."

"Yep, this is definitely a record! 139 inches! It beats the creamed corn back on Aug. 14 by 6 1/2 inches."

"In case you haven't noticed, the Milligans got one of those leaf blowers."

"She's a little cranky when she's tired."

Helen tries out her new "Not-Tonight-Honey" nightgown.

"Jeepers! Is it 12:25 already? A half-hour just isn't enough time for lunch, is it?"

"But the feature that *really* sold us on this vacuum cleaner was its personal hygiene attachments!"

Although they did help to boost attendance at tournaments, the PGA cheerleaders were eventually banned from the tour after repeated complaints from players.

"I had it installed to discourage tailgaters."

Let's face it. Everybody does this when they're assigned a 2,000-word term paper.

"And this is our most popular sofa bed, which we call our 'On the Road Again' model. After two consecutive days of use as a bed, it begins to emit a hideous odor that inevitably persuades tiresome guests to hit the road."

"I don't mean to criticize, but you put those non-slip decals in the tub upside down."

Lloyd Finster was having a tough time adjusting to life as a retiree.

138

"Take the next right."

"Next time ask for paper."

The dream appliance for new parents.

"Here's the problem. The batteries to the garage door opener are in backwards."

"That's the beauty of it! To your average burglar they look like real kids. But they're actually just ceramic dummies with a slot in the bottom for hiding spare house keys."

"I *told* you it was a stupid idea to buy contact lenses at a rummage sale!"

"Personally, I think this new reorganization plan stinks."

"You didn't happen to see the lid to the blender
come through here, did you?"

"I think you've made your point!"

"Oh, for heaven's sake! Don't tell me you were racing against the electric garage-door opener again!"

"They're done! HA HA! *All* the school lunches are done for the next 186 days! No more getting up at 6 a.m.! No more messy sandwiches! No more. ..."

"My! What a good burp *that* was! Let's have one more now."

"And I better not find you kids shaking those presents to try and figure out what they are."

"I wish you'd renew your membership at the health club."

Trick or treating goes high-tech.

The new coffee distribution system not only boosted morale, but it also cut down on time spent mindlessly lingering around the coffee machine.

Coach Wazler discovered that attaching likenesses of players' mothers-in-law to the blocking sled is a powerful motivational tool.

"Here's the problem! The workout tape has been on fast-forward the whole time!"

"I've got the thing wired up to a generator in the basement. We cut our electric bill in half last year."

"The seat that came with the bike was too darned uncomfortable."

A curfew was not something to be taken lightly in the Anderson household.

"...and one for you!"

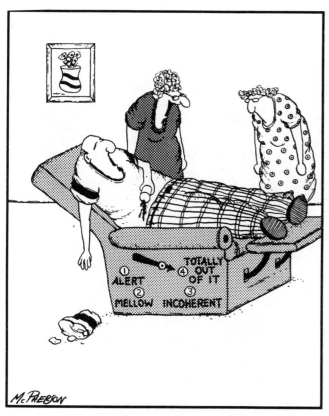

"We must have looked at 50 recliners, but
Al wanted this one because of its
automatic comfort settings."

Though Louise tried to be discreet, people
quickly homed in on the source of the
microwave popcorn aroma.

"So far, five diaper services have canceled us."

"I tell ya, meals used to be such a pain in the neck! Now, thanks to the vending machines, they're a breeze. No more cooking, no more dirty dishes. ..."

"But until we find exactly where the hamster
crawled off to and died, thank heavens for
these little stick-on air fresheners."

"Norm's gotten a little bit lax lately when it comes to cutting firewood."

"Whatever you do, don't tell Mom he's here."

"OK, now the left nostril. Good!"

"I *told* you! I can't do laundry *or* use the stove! The allergy medicine I'm on says not to operate heavy equipment."

"Oh, I forgot to tell you. Your father just installed a security system to warn him anytime somebody sets the temperature above 65 degrees."

"I've been saving us a bundle by buying in bulk!"

"For the last time, Watkins, you can *not* have the day after Thanksgiving off!"

"We're training him to go only on the newspaper."

Not long into the date, Dave began to sense some negative vibes from Glenda.

"I told Ed this was a ridiculous mobile to get a 7-month-old, but he says it's a necessity if she's going to have any chance of getting into Harvard Medical School in 2014."

After spending $30 a square yard for new carpeting, the Schindlers weren't taking any chances.

Although half the team was out with the flu, the Fighting Pigeons of Varnberg High did their best to make their opponents think they were at full strength.

"I need a card that says, 'Sorry I used your new bathrobe to wax the car.'"

"Noreen's having a tough time coping with the Empty Nest Syndrome."

After months of study, management reveals the new reorganization plan.

"I want to apologize to you guys for the little mix-up we've had with the uniforms. I'll be talking to the ballet instructor, and with any luck we'll get things cleared up before the big game on Saturday."

"According to the on-board calorie computer,
you burned the equivalent of three M&M's."

"Well, how did it go at the vet's? Did the cat put up much of a fuss?"

"Don't just shove that back in there any old place! I just alphabetized everything in the refrigerator."

"We know that $2,800 is a lot to spend on a clock, but we couldn't resist once they showed us this engraved signature: 'Ben Franklin, 1752!'"

"Exhale."

"And here you can clearly see the baby's head and ... oh, look! He's wiggling his toes there!"

"So I said, 'I don't care if it's an $800 option. I want the shatter-resistant, soundproof barrier.'"

"Oh, you mean this? My dad's on this big kick lately about making sure we turn out lights when we leave a room."

"He's not much of a watchdog, but he's great with kids."

Hockey in heaven

"For cryin' out loud, will you just give it up
and pay the three bucks?"

"Locked your keys in the house again, eh?"

159

Nobody could clip coupons like
Helen Struman.

"For heaven's sake! Would it kill you to
go out and cut a little firewood?!"

"The computer system is down again."

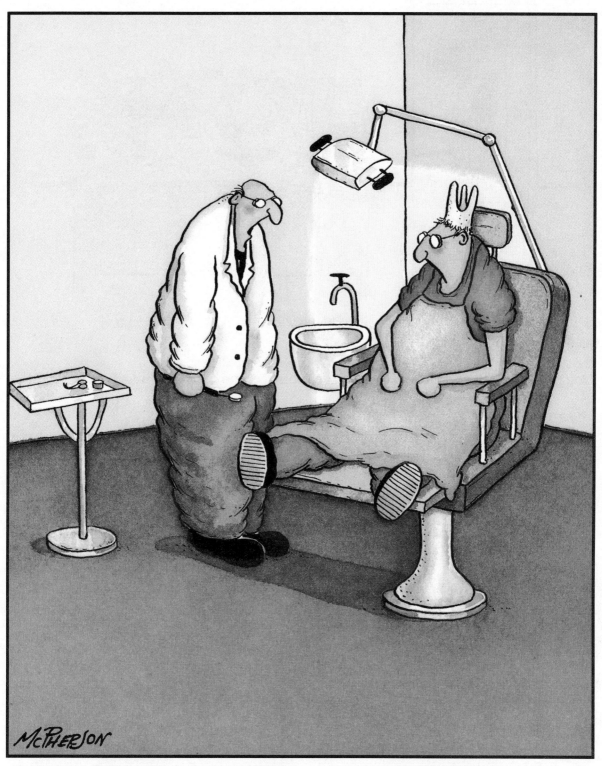

"I'm afraid that wisdom tooth is impacted."

"You guys didn't happen to see my science project come crawling through here, did you?"

"What are you mad at me for? You're the one who bought me this cologne."

"Well, I'd like to see the section in your health book that says pregnant women shouldn't cook!"

"For Pete's sake, watch where you're going! A foot more to the left and you would have put a ski right through my new curtains!"

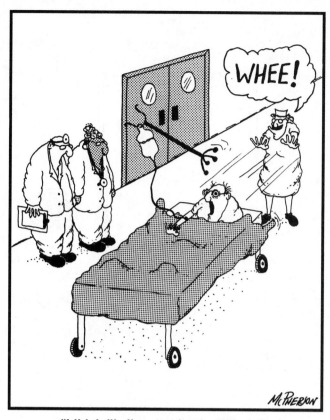

"I think it's time we had a little talk with Nurse Dunn."

Despite his bad back, Wayne held to tradition by making sure his bride was carried over the threshold.

"Isn't there a snooze button somewhere on him that we can hit?"

Although they admired Chuck's dedication, the others in his carpool reminded him that it was 6:49 and perhaps he should start thinking about driving them all home.

"My blow dryer is broken."

"No chance of the cat knocking the tree over *this* year."

"Will you quit buying these darned 'LOVE' stamps? I feel like a hypocrite whenever I pay the electric bill!"

"I lost my whistle."

"Take it easy! It's a clean sock! What'd you expect me to do when we're out of coffee filters?"

"Don found a way to wire the baby monitor into the stereo."

"Looks like that mower of yours starts a little hard."

"Oh look at you! Who says you need a new prom dress?! My old dress fits you perfectly!"

"Looks like Mom and Dad are serious about us not shaking the presents this year."

"It says on your resume that you can type 260 words per minute. No offense, Mrs. Ballas, but I find that pretty hard to believe."

"I told Ed we needed more closet space, so he installed a door made out of Spandex."

"Right now the baby is not in the proper position for delivery, but I'm confident it will shift in time for your due date."

The downside of car pooling

Stella's father should have known better than to try to answer the phone when she was expecting calls from potential prom dates.

"Not only do we know you're not the real Easter Bunny, DAD, you look like a complete bonehead!"

"Oh, yeah? Well, *my* digital watch tells the temperature, humidity, my cholesterol level and blood pressure, and the current Dow Jones industrial average."

"It's part of the company's new emphasis on health and fitness."

Unfortunately for Dominique, neither the Super-Stepper nor the accompanying cassette tape was refundable.

"Lois, go over and help your father get the child-proof cap off the aspirin."

Wendy was starting to sense that her dad wasn't overly impressed with her new boyfriend.

"Boy! That was some pothole!"

"Hey, kids! We've got a lot more string here than I thought! Look at that baby! I'm gonna just keep letting it out!"

"I got sick and tired of putting her in and out of the car seat, so I finally just said the heck with it."

"I realize this may affect your playing, but those darned squeaky sneakers drive me nuts."

"Here's how it works: If the ball hits the floor in your cubicle, you've gotta be on call for the weekend."

"You want your coffee warmed up a bit?"

The new converging conference room walls helped
to keep meetings from dragging on indefinitely.

"Yeah, when we were shopping for garbage disposals, we figured we might as well spend the extra hundred bucks and get the combination disposal/mulcher."

"Bummer."

"Yeah, we used to put out three cans of garbage a week. Since we started composting, we're down to one can."

"I thought the family rental rate was too good to be true."

"Do we still have the warranty for my razor?"

The inevitable result of going for weeks without
untangling your phone cord.

Losing the TV remote control awakened
Bob to the fact that he wasn't exactly
in peak physical condition.

"They say that having a new baby in the house
can be very traumatic for pets, so to help the cats
adjust we've been rubbing catnip on Mikey."

The modern-day widow's watch

"That's my Uncle Vinnie. The organist called
in sick at the last minute."

For people who never remember it's garbage day
until the truck passes their house, Zamco's new
Garbage-Sling 2000 is a must.

"Tommy? He's upstairs in his room
having 'time out.'"

"I'll be going to the Bahamas for a week starting
tomorrow. This should tide you over 'til I get back."

"I think you missed a spot with the sunscreen."

"I'm saving up to get one of those jogging treadmills."

"I thought the tassel looked a little bland so I had it permed."

"Don't be too impressed. It's not real. My kids made it out of Legos."

"We haven't changed those sheets in ages."

"Maybe you haven't heard, Karl, but it's sort of a tradition around here that whoever wins the 50 bucks in the Super Bowl pool takes the rest of the office out to lunch."

"Who did you say did your bypass surgery?"

183

"All right! I think I finally got this
stupid drain unplugged!"

"Could we have separate checks? On one put
me, the woman down there in the weird glasses,
and that kid at the other end putting the straw
in his ear. On another, the guy with the bad
hairpiece, the woman. ..."

"Didn't that pizza delivery kid used to be our paperboy?"

"The coffeemaker is broken."

"Nah, we never clean it out. Once a year we just stick a sign in the yard that says 'Garage Sale.'"

Bob would go to any lengths to get that promotion.

"Let us know if you want a little more leg room back there."

"That's one of the things about living in an old house that drives me nuts. Never enough outlets."

"My baby sitter's got the flu."

"I liked it better when it just beeped when we were overdrawn."

"This'll be a good chance to test that rust-proofing job on the car, huh, Dad?"

Although convenient, having your desk near the coffeemaker has some definite drawbacks.

"I couldn't afford to get airbags as an option. If it looks like we're going to hit something, start blowing these up."

Once again, Wendy beats her curfew.

Budget stress test

"Maintenance says they'll be here first thing tomorrow. They're tied up fixing a leaky toilet over in personnel."

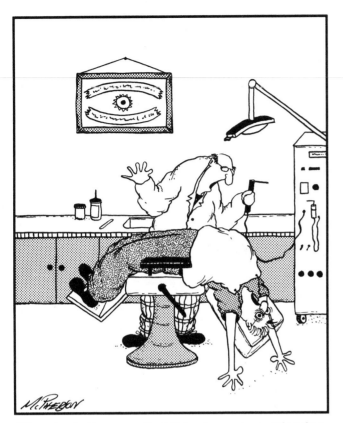

"Hey, look. I'm sorry that this gives you a migraine, but it makes it a heck of a lot easier for me to get to those upper molars."

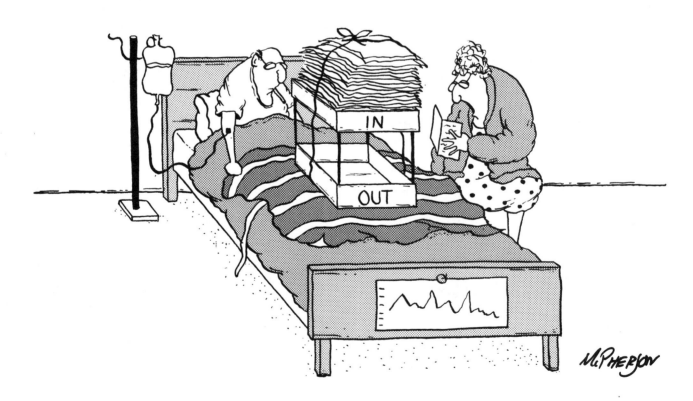

"It's from your boss. It says, 'Best wishes for a speedy recovery.'"

"Well, thank you, Beth Ann! I'll put this up on the
refrigerator right now!"

"Remember the good old days when they were all just called 'sneakers'?"

"As most of you know, the company has undergone some cutbacks recently."

"Looks like I better switch and start using *this* arm to hit the snooze button."

"I don't care if it's a nice-looking vest! It was a sport coat when I brought it in here!"

"You want it set on low, medium, high or industrial strength?"

"I thought of getting a backpack, but they cost a fortune, so I just made outfits for me and Leon out of Velcro and voila!"

"Jim, we've worked together for 17 years. You know I've always respected your opinions, but the entire department, including me, feels you're way off base here. That's definitely Waldo hiding in the coal mine, not in the dump truck, as you keep insisting."

Yet another example of the credit card companies' aggressive attempts to attract new card-holders.

"This is what I get for requesting an office with a window."

"I've been cooking in bulk to save money. Just tell me how much spaghetti you want me to reel off."

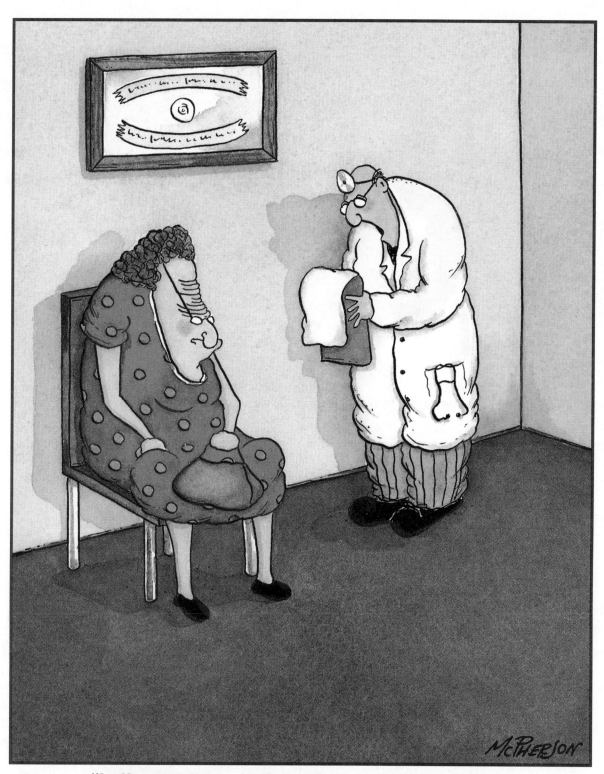

"Let's see now, Helen. You're here for what?
A tummy tuck? No, here it is. A face-lift."

By marking the volleyball with red paint, referees at Pilburn College
were able to avoid heated disputes over line calls.

"Don't expect sympathy from me! I've been telling
you for months that we need a humidifier!"

"Did you ever notice that when you dial your
parents' phone number, it sounds like the
theme to 'The Addams Family'?"

"Granted, it doesn't have the versatility of our other models, but most people find it much easier to play."

"He drank the last cup of coffee and didn't make a fresh pot."

"Hey! You're right! They *are* big jelly beans."

"What d'ya mean this highway is closed? If it's closed, then why on earth
don't they have the decency to warn a person?!"

"Me? A skiing accident."

"Sorry, Dad. We got a little carried away
with the snowman-building."

"My name is Ron and I'm ... I'm ... having a birthday!"

There are times when being a whiz at physics
can be a definite drawback.

"Be sure to compliment him on his wife and kids."

"Oh, for heaven's sake! This thing has been on *reverse* the whole time!"

"Sorry, sir, but something is still setting off the metal detector."

Based on the computer calculations he had run, Lowell needed to hit the ceiling at an angle of 37 degrees in order to land his rubber band in Milt's coffee.

"That's not a twist-off cap."

"I forgot to peel the labels off our glass jars and bottles."

Glenda knew that getting Hal the new Harley Lawn-Pro would be just the motivation he needed to keep the lawn well-mowed.

Hoping to induce phone calls from potential dates, Noreen performs an ancient tribal telephone dance.

"Don't worry, it's not a real tattoo. I just want to see the look on Dad's face when he brings his boss home for tonight's big dinner."

"For God's sake, call a plumber!"

"When you take into account rest stops for me, Louise and the kids, I figure that towing the porta-john will save us about 50 minutes a day."

"Boys will be boys!"

"Sweep it up? What the heck for?
It makes great insulation!"

As the only employees in the office who
didn't have daughters selling Girl Scout cookies,
Ron and Greg were hunted down like animals.

Mrs. Mutner liked to go over a few of her rules
on the first day of school.

"We just locked our baby sitter into an exclusive three-year contract prohibiting her from sitting for anyone else. After that she's eligible for free agency."

"It cost $45, but you shouldn't need to buy deodorant again until you're 68!"

Wayne's latest metal-shop project dramatically changed the course of pillow fights in the Milner household forever.

Being the person who selects a video for the night is a position of awesome responsibility.

"Boy, that was something! I don't know who was more surprised, you or that deer!"

"I've been going over our finances. According to my calculations, our monthly retirement income will be either $2,124 or $42,798, depending on whether or not we win the Publishers Clearing House sweepstakes."

"We discovered that if we reverse the wires and yell into the TV, we can talk to the space shuttle crew."

"Our donations have doubled since we had that thing installed!"

Management felt that the new chart was
helpful in detecting employees who
were abusing rest-room privileges.

"This playpen is good up to age 14!"

"You folks holler if that's too much air for you back there."

Howard offers his opinion regarding the office's
new piped-in elevator music.

"No, really. Be honest."

"Once again, we're very sorry about the mix-up. We can have your furniture here in eight days.
However, we've spoken to the Mulners in Anchorage, and they say they actually prefer
your furniture and are wondering if you're interested in an even swap."

"Have you got that toilet unplugged yet?!"

"I'll take a large pizza with half-onion, two-thirds olives, nine-fifteenths mushrooms, five-eighths pepperoni, one-eighth anchovies, and extra cheese on five-ninths of the onion half."

Bob Swilnard was a lifeguard with an attitude.

211

"I arranged my flex time so that I'll work 14 hours a day, six days a week, and then get 1998 off."

"I told Stan that the ceiling was leaking again, and this was his solution."

"It's times like these that make me hate technology."

"My mother always said, 'You can never have too much counter space.'"

After trying for 25 minutes to get their check,
Ed was finally able to get their waiter's attention.

"The CD player is messed up again."

"I can't believe you cleaned up your entire
room in five minutes."

"And over here we have Tyler's 'Blue Period.'
Notice the strong, sweeping strokes that
seem to leap right off the canvas."

"Wow! That was neat! OK, now try it on high!"

"Good morning, and welcome to
The Wonders of Physics."

One of the hazards of renting a car.

Corporate manager Hank Clemmer firmly
believes that a comfortable employee
is a lazy employee.

After the team lost 20 consecutive games, Coach Farnsworth did his best
to help his players regain their confidence.

"I'm trying to figure out which of these wires carries the
Home Shopping Network so I can cut it."

After hitting seven consecutive shots into
the pond, Rick began to show a hint of
apathy toward his golf game.

Recent advancements in ultrasound technology
have resulted in extremely accurate reports.

"Sorry about this, Mark. My dad has a tendency to be a little overprotective."

"This? This is Ninja Turtle soup."

"I finally decided that the only way to keep the kids' socks straight in the laundry was to number them."

"Sorry about this. My dad wouldn't let me borrow the car."

Aerobics for couch potatoes

"There. Now it's halftime. What do you say we all go to the table and have a nice, quiet Thanksgiving dinner."

It was only July, but already the dreaded
signs began to appear.

Stella knew the importance of being discreet
when making personal phone calls.

Even though they were hard to run in, Don's new shoes made him a serious base-stealing threat.

The latest in couch-potato technology:
the gas-powered recliner.

"I saved the new jumbo slide carousel for last!"